ACCEPTED:

How to Get In to Harvard, MIT, and Other Elite Colleges

A. Jose Rojas, Ph.D.

A. Jose Rojas, Ph.D.
Salisbury University
Salisbury, MD, 21801
CollegeCoachMIT@gmail.com

As a way of saying *thanks* for your purchase, I'm offering a free report that's exclusive to my book readers.

Writing a strong Personal Essay isn't easy for most people but it's an integral component of your college application. The key is to know where to start and how to let your story shine!

In _37 Tips for Writing the Perfect Personal Essay_, you'll discover a variety of tips and tricks to strengthen your application. You will learn how to craft your story and increase your chances of gaining acceptance to your dream school.

This in-depth PDF covers the best practices in Essay craftsmanship and engaging your admissions audience. You can download this free report by clicking here.

CONTENTS

INTRODUCTION: WHY SHOULD YOU LISTEN TO ME?

L et's start with the personal and professional credentials. I was born in Miami, Florida and received my B.S. degree in Chemistry from Georgia Institute of Technology (Georgia Tech) in 2014 where I worked with Seth R. Marder on developing C-H activation transformations and designing new functional materials like organic light emitting diodes and dye-sensitized solar cells. I entered Massachusetts Institute of Technology (MIT) as a National Science Foundation Graduate Research Fellow in 2014 and earned my Ph.D. in chemistry in 2018. My thesis work, with Stephen L. Buchwald and Bradley L. Pentelute, concerned the development of palladium-mediated bioconjugation reactions. During my time at MIT, I was awarded the Dow Chemical Fellowship and Wolf Fellowship from MIT's School of Science. In 2018, I began my independent career as an Assistant Professor of chemistry at Salisbury University. I've published numerous scientific reports that have been cited thousands of times and have developed a myriad of chemical techniques, methods, and synthesized thousands of chemicals for the treatment of HIV, cancer, and MRI contrast agents. I've served on countless admissions committees, both as a student committee member at Harvard University and MIT, and also as a faculty member at MIT, Salisbury University, and Johns Hopkins University. I serve as a peer reviewer for multiple scientific journals and review grants for government agencies such as the National Science Foundation and the National Institutes of Health. I have successfully mentored, coached, and guided many students as they went through the college admissions process and have a lengthy track record of success helping students get into their dream school!

While my formal education is in Chemistry, I'm also passionate about higher education and college. I have taken numerous training courses on evaluating applications, served on boards and committees dedicated to evaluating students for fellowships, scholarships, and other prestigious awards such as Fulbright Fellowships and the Goldwater Scholarship. I have mentored several economically disadvantaged high school students as a mentor and grant-winner of the American Chemical Society's Project SEED, which provides financial support to high school Juniors and Seniors to pursue scientific research opportunities with faculty members at local colleges. While in graduate school I served as a peer mentor for Cambridge, MA's award-winning foundation EnRoot, which provided students in the area with educational support, college guidance, and advice on the college admissions processes.

I participated first-hand in the college admissions process at elite universities and was granted admission as an undergraduate student to Yale University, University of Chicago, and Columbia University. As a graduate school applicant, I obtained admission to Massachusetts Institute of Technology, University of California at Berkeley, University of Texas at Austin, University of Washington, Emory University, and several other elite universities.

I run a college coaching service (link here) dedicated to successfully guiding students through the application process. I have mentored over a hundred students, provided support for families hoping to unlock their child's dreams and potentials. In this role, I've edited personal essays to tailor them for particular colleges and I've helped so countless students gain access to higher education.

What's more, my passion lies in education, generally speaking. I believe that college is the great equalizer for socioeconomic status, can lift people out of poverty, should be attainable by all hardworking children, and I have decided to dedicate my life to ensuring that all students have access to a quality education. This is why I'm currently a college professor and this is why I'm writing this book.

Five fun facts about Higher Education: 1. According to the Brookings Research Center, higher education provides extensive benefits to students, including higher wages, better health, increased levels of life-satisfaction, and a lower likelihood of requiring disability payments later in life. 2. According to US News and World Report, only 0.4 percent of undergraduates attend one of the Ivy League schools. 3. According to the Chronicle of Higher Education, 1.25 million students transferred to another school each year and 1.125 million drop out. 4. Historically, only 2% of Harvard students have flunked out or transferred, according to Harvard themselves. 5. According to the Association of Public & Land-Grant Universities, Bachelor's degree holders make, on average, $32,000 more per year, are 47% more likely to have health insurance, life expectancy is longer by 7 years, and unemployment rates are more than half as low as high school graduates. Clearly, it pays in more ways than just financially to have a college degree.

I legitimately want everyone to have access to a college degree. I'm not a politician or policy maker, so the next-best thing is for me to impart my knowledge of the college admissions process, provide useful information about what admissions committees really want to see, and help you and/or your child unlock all of the benefits of obtaining a degree. Oh, and if they gain acceptance to Harvard, MIT, Yale, Princeton, CalTech, UCLA, Columbia, etc – even better!

I have served on these admissions committees. I have the insider information you're looking for. I WANT to help you! I want to help your child. I want a wiser, smarter, and more educated society. I want everyone (rich, poor, black, white, yellow, brown, orange) to have a shot at achieving their dreams and goals.

This book will unlock the secrets to admissions decisions at elite universities. This book is more than information that you can find on the internet. This book has real stories, about real students, from real college professors, about making real decisions on who gets into colleges. My hope is to breakdown many of the fundamental aspects of gaining admission to your dream school, provide data and statistics to help guide your decisions, and give you the best practices currently in place that ensure you obtain admission to the college you've always dreamed of attending!

CHAPTER ONE: WHAT'S YOUR DREAM SCHOOL?

Not all colleges are created equally. Not all universities have the same course offerings, sure, but each school has a unique culture and your 'fit' for a school does indeed matter. It matters for admissions committees when they're deciding which students to accept, but it also matters for a student's happiness once they begin attending. I've reviewed applications at MIT, a notoriously STEM-focused institution, where a personal essay indicated the student applying was more interested in a liberal arts education. Granted, MIT has wonderful humanities and social science offerings as part of their HASS requirements but perhaps this student would likely be a better 'fit' at a small liberal arts college where they can pursue their creative passions in a vibrant community like Williams College in Massachusetts which is just as prestigious, having been ranked as the #1 liberal arts college by the US News & World report.

Admissions committees rigorously evaluate the personal essays they receive, and I'll go into greater detail about crafting the perfect college admissions essay in a separate chapter. But knowing what school your Dream School is can be more than just a consideration of grades, prestige, rigor, and maybe even fun! In the following pages, I'll break down the different types of colleges that may be of interest to you. Hopefully, you have some idea of what type of environment you'd thrive in and have a general idea of some of the topics you'd like to investigate further in college, as a student. For instance, if you'd like to learn about nuclear engineering, or study philosophy, it's definitely a bad idea to apply to schools that don't offer any coursework in those fields of study! College is not one-size-fits-all, generally. Knowing what schools to apply to is the first step. So, you should create a detailed list of the schools that most align with your interests and passions.

Is a university the same thing as a college? What does phrase "liberal arts" mean anyway? Why are some colleges called private and others called public? Here are the some of the basics on the types of colleges. The first important distinction is public vs. private colleges. Public colleges are typically funded by the local and state governments and often offer lower tuition rates than private colleges, especially for students who are residents of the same state as the college. Private colleges typically rely on tuition, fees, private donors, research grants, or some other external funding source to keep their doors open. For-profit schools also exist outside of this public vs. private distinction and I will not advocate anyone ever applying or attending these types of institutions. These are for-profit colleges are really businesses that offer a variety of degree programs which typically prepare students for a specific career. They tend to have higher tuition costs and fees, which often leads to more debt. Credits earned may not transfer to other colleges, and many are malicious money-hungry institutions that should be avoided at all costs.

There is also a distinction between two-year and four-year colleges. Four-year colleges offer programs that typically require about four academic years that lead to a bachelor's degree. These include universities and liberal arts colleges. Two-year colleges offer programs that last up to two years that lead to a certificate or an associate degree. These include community colleges, vocational-technical colleges, and career colleges. Four-year programs are the ones students generally focus on, but two-year colleges offer many benefits as well, such as lower costs, smaller class sizes, more student support, flexible class schedules, and an opportunity for students to 'ease' into the college experience. Two-year colleges are widely considered to be less academically rigorous, however, so the quality of the institution and whether or not their classes will transfer upon matriculation to a four-year program should be investigated thoroughly. Many two-year colleges have partnerships with neighboring four-year universities and colleges that may provide a smooth transition with measurable benefits to some students and should certainly be considered a viable option for many students. I have witnessed several successful transitions of this sort at elite universities and many of the stigmas against two-year programs are unfounded. Community colleges offer two-year associate degrees that prepare students to later transfer to a four-year college to complete a bachelor's degree.

Liberal arts colleges often are just as prestigious as larger public universities. These liberal arts colleges generally offer a broad base of courses in the liberal arts. This includes areas of study such as literature, history, languages, social sciences, mathematics, engineering, and life sciences. Most liberal arts colleges are private and offer four-year programs that lead to a bachelor's degree. There is a greater emphasis on undergraduate education at these schools, with little-to-no graduate degrees offered. As a result, classes are rarely taught by graduate students and class sizes tend to be smaller with students having direct access to their professors at a greater rate. The education provided at these schools can be steller and generally offer a broader range of study, particularly in the humanities. Because of their smaller size, liberal arts college value close interpersonal interactions between the student body and faculty. The majority of students at liberal arts colleges live at the college. At larger public universities and community college, there are far more commuter students and part-time students.

Universities are usually larger and offer more majors and degree options such as bachelor's master's and doctoral degrees than regular colleges. Most universities contain several smaller colleges within them, such as colleges of liberal arts, health sciences, engineering, education, etc. These colleges also typically have competitive sports teams that compete for NCAA titles.

Vocational, technical, and career colleges may provide the type of education necessary for you or your child. They typically offer specialized training for a specific industry or career. Possible programs of study include the culinary arts, firefighting, law enforcement, medical-record technology, dental hygiene, to name a few. These colleges typically offer certificates of associate degrees. While much of the tips and advice provided in this book can be applied broadly to a variety of institutions, I will focus less on this type of institution going forward.

Single-sex colleges, religiously affiliated colleges, arts colleges, and specialized-mission colleges are colleges that focus on a specific interest or student population. They can also be just as prestigious and academically rigorous as their counterparts. While all four-year public colleges, and most private colleges, are coed, there are some private colleges that only accept men or women. For example, Wellesley College is an example of an all-girl school with a tremendous reputation and notable alumni such as Hilary Clinton. West Point and the Naval Academy in Annapolis are both Officer Training schools that provide excellent education to cadets in a variety of fields such as science and engineering, in addition to traditional coursework. Religiously affiliated colleges, such as Notre Dame, can be quite broad and can also provide an excellent education in a variety of disciplines. These are private colleges with a connection to a particular religious faith. The connection may prove to be only historical and have little-to-no day-to-day effect on student life. Art Colleges and conservatories, such as Savannah College of Art and Design, focus on the arts. They include regular coursework, in addition to training in areas such as music, theater, fashion design, photography, and art design. Most of the colleges in this category offer associate or bachelor's degrees in the fine arts or a specialized field and several offer advanced graduate degrees that can be extraordinarily enriching.

Specialized-mission colleges are also a great opportunity for many students. Historically black colleges and universities, known as HBCUs) focus on educating African American students. Hispanic-serving institutions, or HSIs, are colleges where at least 25 percent of the full-time undergraduate population is Hispanic. HBCUs and HSIs offer programs, services, and activities targeted to the underrepresented students they serve and can provide a comfortable, academically rigorous environment for historically marginalized groups. Many of these colleges, such as Howard University and Spellman College, are well-respected and just as prestigious as their traditional counterparts. These colleges provide a comfortable atmosphere for students unlike more traditional colleges and universities by surrounding the student body with students from similar racial makeups and celebrate their cultural diversity. The Greek life of fraternities and sororities is unmatched at HBCUs and students often report feeling empowered and understood by their cohort and faculty.

Harvard University is what is known as an Ivy League school, but what does being an Ivy League school entail? Most people associate the Ivies with elite universities that are challenging to get into, have rich historical backgrounds, and are home to the most gifted students. The Ivy League, or Ivies, are comprised of eight private schools located in the northeast of the United States. Alphabetically: 1. Brown University in Providence, RI. 2. Columbia University in New York, NY. 3. Cornell University in Ithaca, NY. 4. Dartmouth University in Dartmouth, NH. 5. Harvard University in Cambridge, MA. 6. University of Pennsylvania in Philadelphia, PA. 7. Princeton University in Princeton, NJ. 8. Yale University in New Haven, CT.

Initially, this Ivy distinction started because of a sports conference but it has come to mean much more to students and the world alike. Interestingly, while most commonly associated with elite academics, schools like Stanford, MIT, University of Chicago, etc. are often ranked much higher but the prestige of the Ivies still permeates through various cultures. In addition to the original Ivies, there is also what is known as the term Little Ivies used to refer to a group of small liberal arts colleges in the Northeast. These colleges are Amherst College, Bates College, Bowdoin College, Colby College, Connecticut College, Hamilton College, Haverford College, Lafayette College, Middlebury College, Swarthmore College, Trinity College, Tufts University, Vassar College, Wesleyan University, and Williams College. Like the original Ivies, these Little Ivies are rigorous in academics and admissions criteria. They typically provide more intimate learning environments and are held in high regard.

Due to the prestige of calling an institution an Ivy League school, there are also several other colloquial versions such as the Southern Ivies. These schools are also quite academically rigorous and offer an excellent education from schools such as Duke University, Emory University, Rice University, Tulane University, Vanderbilt University, and Wake Forrest University. These are all colleges of national distinction and often accept some of the most gifted students and sport low admission rates with high selectivity.

Whew! That's a lot of information about schools. It all adds up to be quite a daunting choice and the selection process for deciding which colleges and universities can be overwhelming for many students. We haven't even begun discussing what criteria admissions committees select for and how to tailor your college application list to those criteria. Below is a list of 5 tips to help you decide which colleges to apply to.

1. **Seek out personal recommendations**. A great way to get started finding which colleges to apply to is to speak to those around you. Talk to your counselors, teachers, family, and friends. The final decision should lie with the student, but by crowd-sourcing the decision process, students may be introduced to a spectacular school that they'd never considered previously.

2. **Focus on your goals**. What do you really want out of an educational experience? Do you want to rush, participate in Greek life, and join a fraternity/sorority? Many

schools do not support or condone Greek life so that may eliminate them from consideration. Do you want to go to football games and tailgate? At some schools, sporting events are a prominent part of the college experience and at others they are an afterthought. Do you want to be trained for a specific line of work or do you want a more liberal arts broader education? Do you want to focus on science, technology, engineering, or math? Some schools like M.I.T. or Georgia Tech are science powerhouses but won't be right for students interested in literature and poetry. How does the college rank in the major or field you want to study? The US News & World Report publishes yearly rankings with additional subsets of information in a variety of fields.

3. **Decide where you want to live**. Are you a person who wants to experience big city life, be out in the mountains, have access to a beach, or does farmland pique your interest? Attending Columbia University in the heart of New York City isn't going to provide much open green spaces. Likewise, Stanford University in Palo Alto, California might be too far from home to afford to visit often. Think of yourself as a complete person. There are fantastic schools across the sprawling country, and you want to find a place that you can call home for 4 years.

4. **Visit some schools**. A school brochure and website are designed to attract you. There are teams of marketing experts that work tirelessly to increase their college's attendance with the best and brightest students. As such, relying solely on what you read online or hear from a college rep won't paint the complete picture. There are countless stories of students who attend schools before visiting beforehand who later found out that the culture and environment was completely unexpected from preconceived notions. MIT and Harvard are on the same street in the same city in the same state.

They're both elite universities with outstanding reputations, yet their culture and environment couldn't be more different. You can't just use a ranking or a website to determine if a college is for you. So, schedule some time to go visit the colleges you're interested in before applying. Not only will this provide you to pertinent application information and admission criteria, but you can get a firsthand look at what your life might be like for a significant chunk of time.

5. **Don't fret about money yet**! I speak to high school students that are 14-16 already concerned about affording college. The upcoming crop of students have more pressures and societal worries than perhaps at any time in human history. We'll talk about this more in an upcoming chapter, but before applying, this should not be a primary concern yet. Sure, it is absolutely true that college costs a lot of money, especially with private colleges having exorbitant sticker prices. However, just last year, colleges offered over $100 billion dollars in student financial aid. At Harvard for example, students with families making less than $120,000 per year are given a 'full-ride' – meaning a tuition-free education. Lots of other elite universities have followed suit and offer generous need-based financial aid packages. Besides, you're going to get into an elite university and don't need to worry about your earning potential. A Princeton University degree may cost $240,000 (> $60,000 a year over four years), but the degree you obtain will afford you untold opportunities that are priceless.

As you explore colleges, you may discover that some factors are not as important to you as others. In fact, the whole point of going through this process that I've outlined in this guide is to discover what aspects of college life are going to bring you the great chances for success, joy, and fulfillment. Ultimately, you want to pick a school that allows you to meet your goals, dreams, and career ambitions. Deciding what school is your Dream School may change throughout the course of this process. That's okay. This is an incredibly important endeavor and the investment in your education is worth spending the time to make sure you make the right decision.

CHAPTER TWO:
MAKE YOURSELF
INTERESTING

These are not my words. Former Harvard University President Drew Gilipin Faust presented a talk on how to get into Harvard at the Aspen Ideas Festival in 2014 and said those exact words. "Make your children interesting! We could fill our class twice over with valedictorians." In fact, Harvard has recently been embroiled in a legal battle over grades, test scores, and admissions decisions. In a lawsuit filed on behalf of several foreign students, it has been argued that Harvard's admissions office holds Asians, and Asian-Americans, to a higher subjective standard, rather than relying solely on quantitative assessment measurements. They argue that this limits their admission to the elite Ivy League school and offers admission to weaker students based on a subjective "personal rating" and likability.

While Harvard has denied using such a score, and they say that diversity can only help applicants, Harvard's former President's statements do provide an important lesson. For parents and students alike, they need to know that the single-minded pursuit of academic qualifications such as being on student government, becoming a National Honor Society member, having a perfect 4.0 or higher GPA, taking a smattering of AP classes, and getting untarnished SAT or ACT scores is simply not enough to gain admission to elite universities and colleges anymore. It is certainly essential to present a strong academic track record, but it is not the only measure admissions committees use to evaluate students. In fact, it is becoming increasingly more likely that they take a holistic approach to student evaluation; with some schools abandoning the standardized test requirement altogether.

Schools are ramping up the evaluation of more qualitative measures for success like, passion, perseverance, grit, family hardships, passion projects, varied interests, unique talents or abilities, and a compelling story. While serving on the admissions committee at Harvard, it was learned that the marching band was in need of a new member to play a particular instrument. So, while scouring the field of academically qualified applicants, the committee was tasked with finding a student with a history of playing the tuba at their high school. Of course, this student was gifted academically, but Harvard has hordes of academically gifted applicants every year. What allowed this student to gain admission was more than grades. What do you or your child have to offer that will be of interest to a committee that constantly reviews applications of perfect students? What makes you interesting?

This is not meant to imply that every student needs to run out and learn a new instrument in the hopes of gaining admission to Stanford or Yale because the marching band needs a new trumpet player. It is only meant to reveal the new world of college admissions; your grades and test scores are not the only thing being measured and evaluated against other students. You need to tell a compelling and interesting story. A friend of mine successfully gained admission to Brown University and MIT, in part, because her personal essay was all about her passion for working at a nail salon. She told the story of how much it meant to her growing up, going with her mother for special occasions, how special it made her feel, how the designs fascinated her, how the smell of acetone nail polish remover would bring her back to a special time in place. She wrote about how she wanted to become a chemical engineer and work on developing new and better materials for nails like glue, acrylic, paints, and the like. When admissions committees are combing through thousands of applications each year, the story of academic prowess can become monotonous. My friend's story might seem trivial. But it was well-written, exciting, painted a vivid picture, was interesting and most importantly, it was unique. It made the committee member smile, or perk up, or reminded them of their own passions and dreams. Your job is to do the same.

Obviously, another great story would be hearing about a mission trip to Africa to help starving children. But not everyone has the means to do that. So, what can you do to paint your picture and tell your story? Start with real life experiences and true feelings. Maybe you've always dreamed of becoming a medical doctor, but many of the applicants to these elite institutions have the same ambitious goals that lead to high paying employment. A unique story might be one of becoming a lion tamer or starting a chain of authentic Korean Raman restaurants using organic produce. If your story to tell is that of becoming a scientist or doctor, as so many applicants are, that's fine too. No one is asking you to lie. But it's not going to stand out and you need to stand out next to all the other perfect GPAs and exemplary test scores.

Another friend who went to California Institute of Technology (CalTech) wrote about his experiences on a competitive cheerleading team. CalTech is known as a science and engineering powerhouse and this was a unique story for students that typically apply to this school. In addition to great grades they had a story to tell that was uniquely their own. They talked of being discriminated against as one of the few male members of the team. They wrote about comradery, hard work, leadership, passion, and fun. The story needs to be compelling. The story needs to stand out. Discussing nights spent studying or how University of Pennsylvania has always been a dream school is not very interesting to someone reading the same verbiage for the millionth time. It may be meaningful to you and I don't want to diminish that – but it's not going to stand out to admissions committee. I don't want you to fall into that same trap.

This also means that you need to branch out and explore things besides academics. The story of a student who spends every waking hour studying to achie high grades and ace the SAT is not an exciting tale. You need to develop new skills early on in childhood and pursue those you are most passionate about. Your resume doesn't need to have a TON of activities if you devote yourself deeply into one or two. Don't just pursue a plethora of activities to fill up a stat sheet either. If you want to volunteer, great! But you don't need to do every volunteering opportunity just because you think "it will look good in your college application." Admissions committees would rather see pursued passion that permeates time. We can sniff out the candidates who are merely padding their resume with superfluous and skin-deep schemes. Your pursuits don't even have to be noble for the sake of nobility. If there is a hobby or athletic pursuit that takes up your heart and time, that's fine. Just make sure you can tell a compelling story through those endeavors. And embrace your weirdness. We all have quirks and that is fine. In fact, many elite schools are looking for those bastions of buffoonery. Dressing, speaking, and acting like everyone else can become monotonous. So, if you're a freak, let that flag fly and do it with sincerity and confidence.

Whatever you do, do not lie! Not only can many trained professionals tell when we're being bamboozled or played, but many elite schools have an in-person interview process where these lies will come back to haunt you as a real human probes deeper into your experiences. You need to not only be prepared to write a compelling personal essay with these experiences, but also be prepared to answer more in-depth questions your interviewer may have.

Your personal statement provides the opportunity to tell your story in a way that reveals personal development and self-awareness. Sure, it is an essay that requires the typical format of beginning, middle, and end that ties back to the beginning. But it needs to be more than just following formats. You need to sell yourself to the school and this may be the only opportunity that you have. Below is a list of tips, hinds, and advice for telling a compelling story.

1. **Show, don't tell**. Don't just describe something but really paint a picture with words using vivid details. Don't write "I went to Africa on a mission trip and helped kids." Instead write "I woke to children joyously playing soccer outside my tent in Liberia and to the smell of fresh Liberian coffee being brewed for volunteers of the Peace Corps troupe as we prepared to begin our teaching assignments." It is the vivid details that bring to life a story and make it memorable.

2. **Don't be lazy**. You may be tempted to write a one-size-fits-all personal statement. But each college or university that you apply to may have different prompts. Show that you are conscientious and follow the prompt. Admissions committees can tell that you are recycling statements when you do this. And certainly, don't just change the college name on each essay – heaven forbid you accidentally leave in University of Pittsburgh when applying to Penn State. Each college will ask you specific questions that are slightly different from the other colleges you're applying to. Be sure to be specific and tailor each essay to the prompt and school you're applying to.

3. **Start strong, finish stronger**. Serving on admissions committees, I have read more essays than any human should have to. It gets old and we're human. If you can catch our eye early on with a catchy title or exciting first paragraph, you'll make the process better for everyone involved and increase the likelihood that you get the attention your application deserves. This engages the reader into your story and your world. Read the opening pages of novels you like or notice how articles are written. You've got to have a hook. Students often get a second look and overcome some

of their academic deficiencies with a strong essay.

4. **Focus, focus, focus**. Most students apply to college after walking this earth for 16-18 years. Their experiences are vast, and their personal stories can fill numerous pages. But you have limited space to tell a compelling story and one that is focused on a particular theme is easier to follow and allows you to paint a more in-depth picture. Craft a story in the first person that reveals your unique personality as opposed to the type of student you think admissions committees want to see. Rather than illuminating breadths, focus on depth.

5. **Know your audience and school**. Did you know MIT has a unique hacking culture of pranks that the student body, faculty, and administration all support? Knowing the school you're applying to and the culture of the school is important to showcase that you'd be a good fit and that they would appreciate your contributions to. You should be able to talk about why you like a school more than any other school on the planet and you should make it believable. You should show you've done your homework and understand what makes you an ideal candidate for admission.

6. **Revise, revise, revise**. Use your writing software's tools to catch misspellings and grammatical errors. You want to catch all of these errors before anyone on the admissions committee does. The committees are looking for reasons not to accept you so don't give them one as trivial as a spelling mistake. Have your friends, family, counselors, or teachers read your personal statement. Write a rough draft, revise, and rewrite several times. This process is important and deserves the extra work to make it as well-written and compelling as possible. The saying goes, "every good writer is really a good rewriter." Start early and give

yourself enough time to revise to perfection.

CHAPTER THREE: THE MEASURABLES: GPA AND SAT SCORES

While there are a myriad of components that go into the decision-making process, the one that students and parents spend countless sleepless nights fretting over are the quantifiable measurements colleges use during the evaluation process. These are, you guessed it, grades and test scores. The SAT and ACT test prep services like those provided by Kaplan is a multi-billion-dollar industry; helping students master the exams that they themselves administer and design. Textbooks could be written (and many scientific studies have been!) dismantling the standardized test score as a truly unbiased evaluation method and equalizer of academic prowess. However, to date they are still being used by most colleges to categorize students' worthiness for acceptance into college. One exam, one snapshot of a student's abilities, one day in the life of a complex human being still, unfortunately, holds a tremendous amount of weight to college administrators, students, and parents alike.

Grade point averages are not uniform. Some schools artificially inflate averages, some schools artificially deflate GPAs. Does an A-plus at one school signify the same level of academic rigor as another? Definitely not. Yet, this measurable is still used in almost every admissions decision for aspiring college students around the globe. Additionally, does a B in an Advanced Placement class mean the same thing as a B in an honors class or a B in a general class? Again, it is highly doubtful. It is an imperfect system, and many elite colleges and universities are moving towards a more holistic evaluation of students. Hence, the reason I waited until chapter 3 of this book to go in depth.

Even with the push to look at additional aspects of a student's application during the admissions decision-making process, these quantitative measures still hold a lot of sway with admissions committees. That being said, a few lower course grades, and a subpar standardized test score doesn't always doom students. The published averages at elite institutions may seem high, but it's important for both your sanity and reality that you remember that they are averages, or means, that get reported. This mean some applicants were higher, and some were lower. So, don't consider yourself a hopeless applicant if your SAT score is a few points lower than posted averages or you once got a B in high school trigonometry.

If you do have a particularly checkered academic transcript or past, the personal essay is your chance to discuss why. Maybe you had a bad semester because you had some personal tragedy befall you. Perhaps you had to work full time to support your family and didn't have time to adequately prepare for class. Whatever the case may be, the personal essay is your chance to explain your circumstances. An important note about this explanation is that it should not be an excuse. You should not blame your circumstances but talk about the challenges you faced. Admissions committees hate to see excuses, and definitely don't badmouth your teachers. If you bounced back the following semester with straight A's, use that bump in the road to tell a story of redemption, triumph, and overcoming challenges. Admissions committees love to see improvement over time.

Now, let's talk about grades, test scores, and selectivity. We'll use Harvard as a recent guide given that it is in the title of this book. Harvard, last year, had an acceptance rate below 5.2%.

This means that for every 100 applicants, 5.2 were accepted. Harvard, and other schools in the same echelon are categorized as being 'extremely selective.' Most schools publish their GPA and SAT/ACT averages from their most recent enter classes. Schools love to tout their selectivity because, like a diamond, something scarce and fleeting will increase demand.

Many schools specify a minimum GPA requirement, just to limit the amount of applications they receive to realistic ones. This is often just the bare minimum they publish though, and a more realistic minimum may be a bit higher. Anything below these minimums are typically filtered out as an automatic rejection, and if this is you, you should probably save your application fee money. The GPA requirement that REALLY matters though is the GPA you need to have a shot; the one that gets your essays and complete application in front of selection committees. This is going to be somewhere near the published average GPA for current students.

For Harvard, their most recent class had an average GPA of 4.1. The reason this is above the standard 4.0 for perfection is because most schools use a weighted GPA for Honors and AP classes that can get students above the 4.0 threshold. If your school does not use a weighted system, or even if they use a hyperinflated system, there's no need to be overly concerned or overly confident, respectively. Many institutions also request or calculate unweighted GPAs for their applicant evaluations. That said, it is clear that Harvard places a premium on students being at-or-near the top of their class with nearly all A's in the coursework a student takes. But they look at more than just the average GPA. They also consider what grades came from what classes. An A in an AP or Honors class is going to be held in higher regard and esteem than an A in an elementary-level course. Additionally, if A's are earned in the 'easier' classes but the B's exist solely in the more advanced courses, this may signal that a student is not capable of the rigor required to succeed at Harvard, or whatever college is evaluating the applicant.

If you're currently a junior or senior, your GPA is difficult to change much in time for college applications. If there are deficiencies in this area, they can be made up for in other areas. For example, competition or research experiences in science fields may help alleviate concerns about a poor chemistry or biology high school grade. This is true of any component of your application. It is not the expectation that all students must be perfect in every aspect of their story. But they must exemplify excellence in at least some of the components to make up for other deficiencies in their application. The SAT or ACT is another measurable which can help overcome lower-than-average GPAs. Especially in the areas that align. For example, a perfect math score on the SAT may help assuage the admissions committees concerns about a B in an algebra course. In short, if you have a lower GPA than the average, you'll need a higher SAT or ACT score to compensate for that.

Each school has different requirements for standardized testing. Most schools still require some form of standardized testing such as the SAT or ACT and some even require SAT subject tests. Harvard for example, definitely requires either the SAT or ACT, and they require a high school. While many schools say that they do not have an SAT score cutoff, this is simply disingenuous. The 'hidden' SAT requirement likely lies somewhere slightly below their average scores for recently accepted students. For example, on the 1600 SAT scale currently being used (sometimes referred to as the New 1600 SAT), Harvard had a recent entering class with an average of 1520. The 25th percentile of the New SAT score has been reported to be 1460. This means that if you score a 1460 on the New SAT, you are listed as below average. The 75th percentile for the New SAT has been reported as 1590.

The reason these standardized test scores are losing their luster (at least insofar as school's will admit publicly) is because of the billion-dollar test prep industry. If you have access to test prep guides, study courses, or tutors, you should certainly take advantage of them because it has been proven scientifically that they do in fact lead to higher scores on these exams. But what this also means is that if you don't have the means financially to afford these test preparation services, you are at a disadvantage. This truism has led many in the field to cry for eliminating the practice altogether. In fact, even the test-administering bodies in charge of these exams have taken notice and tried to put in place socioeconomic balance checks to mitigate these concerns. This is a new development and it remains to be seen if it will have any impact. What does remain a fact though, is that even though elite institutions know this, they have been slow to react and still regularly use standardized test scores from the SAT and ACT to evaluate students and help make admissions decisions. If any true sweeping changes are made, I will update this section. But as of 2020, the SAT and ACT should be considered an important component of the application for every student.

An additional consideration for the SAT is what is known as their SAT Score Choice Policy. The policy at each school is an important part of the testing strategy. Harvard has the Score Choice policy of "Highest Section." Another common phrase for this is "superscoring." Superscoring, or Highest Section allows students to choose which SAT tests to send to a school, if multiple attempts are made on an exam. Of all the scores Harvard receives when utilizing this method, the application readers will only consider the highest section scores across all SAT test dates you submit. The SAT and ACT are not inexpensive, but if you have the financial means to take advantage of multiple attempts, this method of scoring can only help the student. For example, if a student takes the SAT exam 3 times and scores a 300 on the math section the first time, a 750 the second time, and 475 the third attempt, only the 750 "superscore" will be presented to admission committees. You can take the exam as many times as you'd like and submit only the tests that give you the highest superscore.

That said, it is strongly recommended that you take this exam very seriously, give yourself ample time to prepare, utilize every resource you have available. Take practice exams, read books, attend SAT prep courses and test yourself under similar conditions to test day. Another strategy some students have taken with some success is to focus all of their attention and study efforts on one section at a time to maximize their superscore. An ideal scenario would be an exemplary score on the first attempt, but if that is not your situation, you should continue to try and improve this score as much as you feasibly can.

Like the SAT, Harvard will also evaluate the ACT similarly. The average ACT score of accepted Harvard students is a 34. The 25th percentile for the ACT is 32 and the 75th percentile is a 35. Also like the SAT, they say they don't have a cutoff score, so it is best to be near their posted averages. Harvard also uses a similar "superscore" methodology to evaluate only the highest sections for all exam attempts. One more important note about "superscores:" not all schools practice this same method of evaluation and compute superscores. Some schools look at every exam taken and will instill their own unique method of evaluation. This is another reason each student should take their first attempt seriously and aim to achieve their highest score possible every time they take the exam.

But wait, there's more! What about subject specific tests? The SAT and ACT both have a Writing section that includes an essay for submission. Harvard, and most other selective schools, require the SAT/ACT writing section for a complete application. They will use this as another factor in the evaluation process. Maybe liberal arts schools place a heavy focus on this section and if your intended major is in the humanities, a strong Writing score will improve your chances of admission. In recent years, science heavy schools have also begun evaluating this section more strictly as they aim to combat that idea that scientists are poor communicators.

Schools vary in the other SAT subject test requirements. Typically, the most selective schools will require them, but some do not. You should do your research to determine if the schools you intend on applying to require subject-specific SAT/ACT tests. Harvard, for example, has indicated that SAT subject tests are required for admission. Typically, the standard SAT/ACT and GPA scores are the most heavily weighted measurables, but you do still have the opportunity to improve your application, or destroy it, based on the SAT Subject Tests. While the main focus of your studies and anxiety should be on improving the standard exams, the subject tests should not be ignored.

With all of this being said, your admission decision will not rely only on your GPA or SAT/ACT scores. Your coursework difficulty, extracurriculars, personal essays, and letters of recommendation will be considered heavily. Especially at extremely selective schools like Harvard, most applicants fall around their reported averages and the other components of an application can truly separate a student positively or negatively for admission consideration. Additionally, different schools place different emphasis on each component of the application. Research into each school's admission criteria tends to vary year to year, but a good starting place can be found in the historically reported data on their websites or through an aggregator such as US News & World Report.

One last note, while I chose to focus on Harvard's typical accepted applicants, the values reported here are relatively similar across other elite institutions of similar prestige. For example, CalTech's average SAT is 1560, Princeton is 1500, MIT is 1528, and Rice University is 1535. Again, it's important to remember that these are just averages so if your score lies slightly outside of these values, don't fret. Plenty of students are accepted with lower exam scores and GPAs, especially when another component of their application is particularly strong. It's okay to have 1 or 2 deficiencies, so long as the entire application is compelling and impressive.

How do you get a perfect ACT or SAT score? The maximum score on the SAT is currently 1600. In order to get this type of score you need to do the following: miss less than 1 or 2 questions on the reading section, get every question correct on the math section, and miss less than 1 or two questions on the writing section. Below is a list of tips, tricks, and proven methods for showcasing your academic prowess on these standardized tests.

1. **Work hard AND smart**. This should go without saying but diligence, perserverance, and many hours spent studying and taking practice tests is the one consistent factor in students who attain perfect scores on standardized tests. There's more to it than that, but this factor cannot be understated. Under no circumstances should the test day be the first time a student takes a version of this test. They should have spent many hours preparing. You need the motivation to push yourself and continue to improve on practice scores. You need to devote time to studying vocabulary, answering math questions, and actively practice essays for the writing section. However, deliberate practice is essential. Meandering through the study process for the sake of increasing study hours is a low impact practice. High impact practices include selecting proven and high-quality practice materials. Understanding how questions are framed and presented will allow you to recognize patterns and attack problems in similar ways as you gain experience and expertise. Obtaining official SAT practice tests directly from the College Board is the best way to do this. Most students report taking over 10 full-length practice tests before ever taking the real test on exam day.

2. **Start studying early**. One of the first questions typically ask is when to start preparing to take the SAT or ACT. How much you need to improve will determine how much you need to study to achieve your goal. It is always recommended to begin by taking a practice SAT or ACT score, which you can find online for free. Be sure to take the exam by simulating real testing conditions to get an accurate assessment of your current preparedness. A rough guide on how much studying will lead to point improvement is as follows: a. 0-30 point improvement is 10 hours of study b. 30-70 point improvement is 20 hours of study c. 70-130 point improvement

is 40 hours of directed study d. 130-200 point improvement is 80 hours of study and anything more will likely require greater than 150 hours of study.

3. **Use official practice tests**. The best questions to study from are those that most resemble the real exam. The SAT and ACT are very unique in their structure and the College Board has many official practice exams available for purchase. You can also likely find some online or through your school but using 'fake' practice exams won't be very useful. A tremendous flaw of many test prep books is their practice questions don't accurately resemble the real test. They are usually either much more difficult or much easier than those you'll find on the SAT or ACT. Also, the formatting may be different and there are test psychology studies that show practicing using the same format makes students more comfortable on test day and reduces test anxiety.

4. **Attack your weaknesses with data**. Focusing on WHY you're missing questions and trying to improve on your weaknesses is an effective strategy for improving your scores. If you just do a ton of practice questions but don't stop to analyze WHY you're getting questions wrong, your scores won't improve. If you want to ace these tests, you'll have little room for error. You need to understand all the different types of questions and be able to finish the exam in the allotted time. A sound strategy is to mark each question that you're unsure about and upon review, thoroughly examine each of those question types that you get incorrect or guessed on. Once learning the correct answer, really try to find out WHY it is the correct answer and where your mental mistakes arose from. Keep track of these questions and revisit them in the future. If you find that certain topics are consistently giving you trouble, take some time to review that material with a textbook, Khan Academy videos, or ask a teacher or mentor to help

you review. The exam is also timed so you'll need to be able to complete the questions efficient and effectively under time constraints. Always make sure to time yourself on the exam sections and if you notice yourself taking more time on certain questions, figure out why and try to speed up without diminishing your results.

5. **Answer everything, even if you're unsure**. Before the redesign of the SAT exam in 2016, incorrect answers were penalized, and it was recommended to leave blank questions you were unsure of. That is no longer try and there is no penalty for incorrect answers, so it is in your best interest to answer every single question, even if it's a guess. Try to eliminate answers that obviously incorrect to increase the statistical probability of selecting a correct answer when guessing. If you're efficient with your time, you should have the opportunity to answer every question with thoughtful consideration. However, if you come to the end of the timed exam and have several blank questions, you should still fill in random bubbled answers to give yourself a chance of getting extra right answers.

CHAPTER FOUR: COMMON APPLICATION, UNIVERSAL COLLEGE APPLICATION, OR COALITION APPLICATION

When applying to elite colleges and universities, many have begun using 3 portals to evaluate their applicants. You may apply through one of these 3: The Common Application, the Universal College Application, or the Coalition Application. For most applicants, it is recommended to utilize the Common App. You can and should apply as early as possible for the great likelihood of sufficient evaluation. These dates are typically Early Action around November 1st of each year or Regular Decision by January 1st. In the next chapter we'll discuss which of this admission options are best for you. Here, we'll focus on the different application types and which to use for which schools.

College applications take a lot of time and effort to complete. The sheer volume of information you're expected to provide that covers every aspect of a child's life can be quite overwhelming, especially when multiplied by the 7, 10, 20, or sometimes 50 schools students apply to for a given cycle. Much of this information is ridiculously repetitive. Every college needs to know your address, who your parents are, your SAT scores and GPA, etc. It's even likely that you'll use the same letters of recommendation for every college you apply to. Some schools even have the same essay questions or personal essay expectations. This is where the Common Application, Universal College Application, and Coalition Application flexes their strength.

Colloquially known as the Common App, this system streamlines the college application process by letting students apply to any of its hundreds of member schools through a common portal. The basic application is automatically uploaded into each member school's application after entering it in just a single time. Most colleges choose to require additional supplemental information such as questions, writing prompts, or other requirements that will require tailoring to specific institutions, but at least some of the busy work is removed. All of the portals listed above provide the same basis of automatically populating the redundant information.

It's best to get acclimated to the system and begin entering information into the system well before the application deadline dates and the online portals all 'go live' well before these deadline dates. I generally recommend using the Common App because most of the schools you'll want to apply to use it, including all 8 Ivy League schools, Stanford, MIT, and hundreds of other elite institutions use it. While some admissions professionals have criticized the Common App for being too generic, there is no argument to be made that it simplifies the application process for both colleges and students alike. What's more, many international schools such as Oxford University or the Swiss Institute of Technology have begun to accept applications submitted through the Common App. As of 2013, the option to mail in your application has been discontinued and the application must be completed on the Common App website, electronically.

Once you've determined that you will be using the Common App to apply to multiple schools, you need to gain comfort navigating the website. You can find a list of all the schools that accept the Common App form of applications online (there are over 700 schools) and if there is a school not listed, you will need to follow that school's individual application process. Once creating an account and selecting the colleges you play to apply to, the Dashboard on their website does a good job of listing each college's unique requirements. They even track your completion progress for each individual school, making it easier to keep track of all the information necessary for a complete application. It is important to note that the Common App website will not submit your applications until you have completed the entire checklist for that school, but you don't need to be complete at EVERY school before submitting. It may take a long time to complete each application for each school so you should work diligently and systematically to ensure completion. I suggest organizing this either from easiest to hardest or from most important to least important. For example, if Harvard is your dream school, you should definitely spend the most time and first allotment of time completing their application. Contrary to popular belief, it is important to submit early. Over the course of the evaluation process, the admissions committees often give their full attention earlier on in the process – we're human and get tired just like everyone else. It also makes it harder to stand out after reading several hundred applications and as I've mentioned in a previous chapter, you need to stand out!

The supplements section of each college that you've added to the "My Colleges" section is where you'll find writing prompts or other submission criteria unique to each school. Always be sure to read carefully and submit the materials requested in the formats requested. Many institutions will immediately dismiss your application if you don't follow the directions correctly. We are going to be too busy to go out of our way to make your submissions fit and it shows a lack of conscientiousness that admissions committees attribute to successful applicants. So be careful and take your time formatting and proof reading all of your application materials. It's a trivial matter that will only hurt you if done incorrectly. Reviewing the My Colleges tab is a great way to keep track of admissions information for the various schools that you're applying to, but unfortunately it does not cover all the terms and details of each school's admissions practices, so it is not a substitute for more in-depth research. Under each school in the My Classes tab, there is usually a link to view college website in the contact section where you can visit the admissions website of that individual school and find out more about their policies and requirements. If you're ever unsure about how to answer some of the required questions, you can visit the "Instructions and Help" section of the Common App website or ask your guidance counselor at school.

The College Search section is your portal into the Common App's database of member schools. You can use this section to search among the colleges that use the Common App for schools that meet your particular criteria and to learn more about those schools. You can also use this section to add colleges to your college list to appear on your Dashboard and you My Colleges section.

Once you're ready to submit the Common App, you'll need to thoroughly go over your application to make sure that you've answered all the questions adequately and filled in all the blanks. Take your time because there are no take backs when submitting these applications. The Common App will notify you if you've left any of the required sections unanswered or if there are errors. It is best to look it over yourself though and even consider having someone else proofread and ensure that all of the information you've entered is correct. To start the submission procedures, go to your My Colleges section, you'll choose your letter of recommendation authors and sign the FERPA waiver. At this point, you'll click "Review and Submit – Common App" under the application heading. The system will redirect you to submit your application fees directly to each individual college that you've selected (if you qualify for the Common App waiver, you will not have to make a payment at this point). Once submitting the application fees, you'll sign and date your application and hit "Submit" on your Common App.

For most schools, this is not the end of the process. You're going to be required to submit several school-specific writing supplements separately and you cannot do so until your Common App has been submitted. This is another reason to submit early because it may take you some time to complete each school's supplemental requirements. To submit these writing supplements, you'll click on "Review and Submit Writing Supplement" under the heading and the process will be similar to other sections in the Common App. Simply follow the instructions given by your particular school. Once submitted, you should ensure that it has went through correctly by navigating to the Dashboard within the Common App account and look for the school to which you submitted the writing supplement. If done correctly, you'll notice a green checkmark across from that school's name under the Application column. You'll still need to ensure that your official test scores and recommenders submit their documents before your application is truly complete. And, sadly, you'll need to repeat this same submission process for each of the colleges you wish to apply to. It can be quite repetitive, but much of the information for each school will be similar and this information will simply be auto-populated into their sections.

Once your application is complete and you begin the process of submitting it to a college, you can download a PDF of your application in the print preview form to review your application. You should definitely consider keeping these applications for your records because you may be asked about your question answers later on at an interview or by one of the school's faculty or staff.

Below is a list of the different sections of the Common App and how to fill them out.

1. **Profile**. In this section, you'll enter detailed information about yourself. It is divided into sections covering a variety of topics such as your contact information and your citizenship. The title bar of each section is gray bar and will open up an answer box or checklist for you to submit. This section also has a fee waiver request form which you can use to avoid the expensive application fees if your family income meets the required threshold. Each college has pretty high application fees that may be a factor when deciding which colleges and how many colleges to apply to. You should utilize this tool if you even have an inkling that you may qualify.

2. **Family**. In this section, you'll answer questions about your family, such as your parents or siblings. As before, you'll click on the title in the gray bar for each section in order to open it and answer its questions. This section will also ask where your parents went to college, which is a factor at some schools when evaluating applicants. Some colleges actively seek out the children of alumni for admission, but some schools are anti-nepotism.

3. **Education**. In this section, you'll answer questions regarding your educational experiences such as what schools you've attended, your GPA, scholastic achievements, your educational attainment goals, and courses you are now taking or have recently taken. You should fill out as many scholastic achievements as you can, regardless of how mundane you may think it is.

4. **Testing**. In this section of the Common App, you'll need to decide whether or not to self-report your standardized test scores and possibly future test dates in addition to sending official score reports directly to the colleges you're applying to. You can self-report to the Common App whichever tests you'd like to report your scores for, and then enter your scores for those tests.

5. **Activities**. In this section, you'll be entering all of the

activities you participated in as a high school student. You can add up to ten activities and you'll be asked a number of questions about each one. These questions will include when you participated in the activity, how much time per week you spend engaged in this activity, and your notable accomplishments or leadership positions associated with that activity. This is the section to highlight your story and make your meaningful activities really shine to the admissions committees. You don't need to feel obligated to fill out all 10 of the activities. Remember, admissions teams care more about depth than breadth.

6. **Writing**. In this section, you're going to answer questions that require longer written responses, starting with your personal essay. Under the "Personal Essay" section you'll find a list of topics to choose from and a box in which to copy and paste your essay text. It is strongly recommended that you compose your essays and writing prompts in word to ensure your grammar and spelling is perfect and pasting it into the text boxes. When doing this, ensure that the formatting isn't destroyed and that it is still easy to read and follow. The writing section also has a section under "Disciplinary History" where you'll be asked if you have been found responsible a disciplinary infraction either at school or in the community. This section gives you an opportunity to address or explain what happened. Lastly, there is also a section under "Additional Information" where you can include information on any special circumstances that may be pertinent to your application but are not addressed elsewhere on the Common App.

CHAPTER FIVE: WHAT THE BEST SCHOOLS LOOK FOR

Harvard publishes an article on their website every year titled "What We Look For." Many other elite colleges and universities publish similar types of articles on their school's admissions site and you should take a look at a few during your preparation process. I think you'll find, like most people do, that most colleges are looking for the same type of student. During the admissions process, Deans and administrators have instructed admissions committees to select for a particular type of applicant, albeit broadly, and this has a huge impact on what type of students gain admission to these schools. These criteria tend to vary from year to year, however, only slightly. Generally speaking, what follows is a solid guide to the type of student that prestigious colleges will hope to offer admission. Colleges are seeking to identify students who will become the best educators of one another and their professors – these are individuals who inspire the people around them. These are students who inspire during their time at the institution and who will continue to inspire and lead after graduating.

1. **Growth and Potential**. Ask yourself the following ques-

tions: Have you reached your maximum potential as a student and on a personal level? Have you been extending yourself broadly enough to reach your potential? Have you been spending your time wisely on academic, employment, or research pursuits? What are you doing with your 'free time?' Do you have more left in the bank that you can provide? Have you identified your goals and passions or are you exploring more in hopes of actively finding it? Do you have some sort of initiative or direction? What motivates you to achieve your goals and dreams? Where do you want to be in 5, 20, or 50 years? Will you contribute something meaningful to the world? What sort of human are you now and what sort of human will you be for the rest of your life?

2. **Interests and Activities**. Do you care about anything so passionately and deeply that you can't stop yourself from pursuing it? It doesn't matter if these are intellectual pursuits, personal, or extracurricular but you need to have them! What have you learned from the experiences you've already had and how have they shaped your future pathway? With the interests you do have, how have you pursued them and what successes or failures have you had that taught you lessons? What is the quality of the things you've already done, and do you appear to have a genuine commitment or leadership role? If you haven't had a ton of experiences due to some circumstance that's been holding you back, what do you hope to explore at the school that you would otherwise never have the chance to?

3. **Personal Character**. What choices have you made for yourself based on your beliefs and why have you made them? Are you a late bloomer, early starter, or consistent pursuer? How open are you to new ideas and people? What about your maturity, character, self-confidence, leadership, energy, concern and grace under pressure, or energy is a positive influence on the world?

4. **Contribution to the School's Community**. Will you be able to stand up to the pressures of college life? What about the freedoms afforded to you living away from your familiar world? Will you contribute something meaningful to your class and your school, and if so, what will that be? How do you know? Would students benefit from being around you? Will the school benefit and grow due to your presence? Would another student be lucky to be your roommate? Would your professor be lucky to have you as a student? Would someone be lucky to be on the same team as you? Are you willing to collaborate and build with others?

These questions above allow admissions committees to give deliberate and meticulous consideration of each applicant holistically. You should be prepared to answer questions like these in your personal essay, during interviews, and present your application in such a way that answers these questions even without ever being prompted. If you don't answer these questions over the course of your entire application's unique fields of inquiry, then you will not be considered for admission to your dream school because you haven't completely told your story. These are the things admissions committees are looking for because a stellar GPA or perfect SAT score is not enough to stand out. It might be enough to be valedictorian at your high school, but every Princeton student or Harvard student or Yale student was their high school's valedictorian.

A.L.D.C's is another acronym that you should become familiar with because, while it has previously been shrouded in secrecy, it has recently been revealed to carry a lot of weight in the admissions process at elite schools. It turns out that these prestigious universities give advantages to recruited athletes (the A), legacies (the L), applicants on the dean's or director's interest list (the D), and the children of faculty and staff (the C). Legacies are children or family members of prominent alumni from the university. Applicants that fit the D bill tend to be children of extremely wealthy donors and prominent people. Recently, it has been reported by the New York Times that while ALDCs make up only around 5% of a school's applicants, they account for about 30% of all admitted students. The typical acceptance rate at prestigious schools hovers around 5-10%, but for ALDC-type applicants, this acceptance rate rises closer to 50% representing a distinct uptick. If you have any such affiliation to the school, it will help, and you should feel completely warranted at drawing attention to your unique standing.

Another type of student that has a distinct advantage of other applicants with similar GPAs and test scores are students from sparse parts of the country. There are about 20 states in the United States that are largely rural and have relatively few applicants that apply to places like Harvard, Yale, and Princeton. But haven't you noticed that every school likes to tout how they have students from all 50 states and various countries? If these schools want to maintain their ability to make such proclamations but only receive 2 applicants from North Dakota, there is a strong likelihood that at least one of those students get accepted. If you are from one of these states, or can claim so on an application, you should utilize your advantage. In fact, Harvard might even actively recruit applicants from these places once they receive PSAT scores that are higher than their unpublished cutoffs.

Effervescent or unusually appealing personal qualities increase the likelihood of acceptance into prestigious schools. The recent Harvard lawsuit unveiled a lot of information regarding their admissions practices and it was found that students with "unusually appealing personal qualities such as charity, maturity, and strength of character" are often sought out for admission at higher rates.

Navigating all of these qualities that the best schools are looking for can be challenging. Most applicants think that they just need the best test scores and grades and take the hardest classes. In truth, elite institutions are drowning in those kinds of applicants and are seeking much more well-rounded applicants and evaluating their character even more stringently. As evidenced directly from former Harvard Dean Bill Fitzsimmons in a 4-part piece in the New York Times, "Efforts to define and identify precise elements of character, and to determine how much weight they should be given in the admissions process, require discretion and judiciousness. But the committee believes that the "best" freshman class is more likely to result if we bring evaluation of character and personality into decisions than if we do not." He goes on to add, "While there are students at Harvard who might present unusual excellence in a single academic or extracurricular area, most admitted students are unusually strong across the board and are by any definition well-rounded. The energy, commitment, and dedication it takes to achieve various kinds and degrees of excellence serve students well during their college years and throughout their lives."

CHAPTER SIX: THE INTERVIEW

Many elite colleges are now requiring or strongly recommending applicants to go through an additional process known as the college interview. This interview can take many forms, take place in a variety of locations, and be conducted by a variety of people affiliated with the school. They can take place in informal locations like coffee shops, libraries, or more formally on the campus itself, or at your hometown school. While your GPA, test schools, personal essay, and writing samples will likely hold much more weight than the typical college interview, it is still an integral component of the evaluation process and should be taken seriously with ample preparation. What follows is a guide on how to prepare for these interviews and some examples of things you can expect to encounter during your time with the interviewer.

First and foremost, you should prepare questions to ask your interviewer about the school, student life, and what makes their institution so special. You'll need to talk about why you want to go there, but you should also ask questions that let you know why you should go there as well. You should put some energy into coming up with creative questions with answer's that cannot be easily found on the school's website. If you have a current student, or recent alum, as your interviewer, you can ask them about what parts of their experience beyond academics that made their experience so special. You should also use this opportunity to learn more about the nuances of the school. Hopefully your excitement will exude naturally because, after all, this is your dream school and any opportunity to learn more about it should raise excitement levels.

Being interviewed is a skill that doesn't come naturally to many and you should practice. You should practice with a guidance counselor, your parents, classmates, or really anyone with any sort of experience with the interview process. Have your practice interviewer ask you their best typical college questions and be prepared to share stories of your past experiences. Common powerful answers include stories of overcoming obstacles, showcasing strong character, and discussing achieving your goals through your exquisite work ethic. Answer honestly and also ask your practice interviewer to critique your responses. Interviewers are people and will feel more comfortable if you come off as comfortable. Hopefully your interviewer is pleasant, friendly, and personable, but also ask them to interview you in a way that is the complete opposite. Occasionally, interviewers will be stone faced and off putting in order to test you and see how you react to uncomfortable situations. Remain positive and excited about the prospect of learning more about the school.

Common interview questions you might expect to be asked include, "Why do you want to attend this college or university?" Great answers include specific examples. Your interviewer likely wants to be as excited you are and reminisce about their college experience. "What's your favorite subject in school?" "What do you want to study in college?" If you don't know specifics, that's okay! But just make sure you talk about being excited about the school's offerings and the opportunity to find your passions at a school that challenges you and opens doors for you. "What do you enjoy doing when you're not in class? What are some interesting things I wouldn't know from your application?" Most interviewers if they are students or alumni might only have access to limited information from your application due to FERPA reasons. So be prepared to elaborate and expound upon some of the things you mentioned in your application but you should also be prepared to share more stories and information about those experiences. "What's an example of an obstacle, a failure, or a mistake you learned from?" This one is particularly important because it showcases learning experiences on a personal level while also giving you the opportunity to showcase the strength of your character. Try to choose an example or story that is more than just getting a good grade in a challenging class. That's boring and interviews want to hear more interesting stories. Be yourself but be your best self.

While it may be true that you have some deficiencies, insecurities, and faults, you don't want to leave that impression with your interviewer. You want to find the best fit for your interests and personality and the interviewer will have a better handle on that information. Ask them about the students and culture and environment of the institution and find ways to showcase how you'd be an excellent addition to the student body. Don't show up looking like you don't care about the interview but feel free to dress with hints of your personality. You don't necessarily need to wear a suit, but you don't want to be off putting either.

Most interviews last between 30 minutes to an hour but don't look at the clock. Sometimes they'll be longer or shorter and you shouldn't read into that. Some interviews are scheduled back to back, but some interviews have a ton of leeway in the schedule. If you notice your interviewer checking the clock, you also shouldn't read into that because they may have other obligations and plans. Just go with the flow on the time component.

Should you send a thank-you note? I think yes and I always appreciate receiving them. At the very least, you should send a thank-you email but the personal touch of a card, particularly one that mentions specifics of the meeting, is always a nice touch. If there was something about the interview that was particularly helpful or insightful, you should let your interviewer know. If you connected over a book or song or experience, you can mention it. If not, simply reiterate your interest in the school and thank your interviewer for their time. Most of the time, interviewers are volunteers who are only participating because they love their former school and want to ensure that its future is in good hands with new students.

If you have the option, but aren't necessarily required to interview, you should take advantage of this benefit. It is an opportunity to show the school how passionately interested you are in attending. Your excitement will be infectious, if genuine, and will increase your chances of gaining acceptance. Under no circumstances should you display melancholy. Do whatever it takes to put yourself in a good mood before the interview. While not everyone needs to be happy all the time, it is a truism of psychology that people are affected by the mood of those around them. If you're positive and happy, it may influence your interviewer to also be positive and happy when writing their review of the experience.

Below is a list of additional interview questions that I have asked, been asked, and others have shared with me during their interview experience:

1. **Tell me about yourself.**
2. **Why are you interested in this school?**
3. **Tell me about your strengths.**
4. **Tell me about your weaknesses.**
5. **What do you think you can contribute to this school that they don't already have?**
6. **What do you expect to be doing 10 or 20 years from now?**
7. **What would you change about your high school?**
8. **What was the best part of your high school experience?**
9. **Who do you most admire?**
10. **What's your favorite book?**
11. **Who is your favorite musical artist or band?**
12. **Why do you want to go to college?**
13. **How have your parents or other family members influenced you?**

14.What do you like to do for fun?
15 How did you persevere to overcome an obstacle?
16.What makes you unique?

For each of these questions, it's important to be prepared to provide information that helps your interview learn about how unique and interesting and full of character you are. Don't try to write out your answers completely and memorize them because you don't want to seem robotic, but you should definitely have a general idea to disseminate. Practice your responses by having someone ask you these questions and more and try to answer them as you would in an interview. Be as detailed and specific as you can with your responses. You really want to paint a vivid picture with words for your interviewer to remember and be transported to the experience. Learn to do this, and you will truly begin to separate yourself from other applicants that are undergoing interviews.

For some of these questions, it may behoove you to review your personal statement that you submitted to the school. Your personal statement can act as a guide to help you incorporate some information into your answers and provide you the opportunity to expand on those shared experiences. Undoubtedly, the questions above don't provide you with all the possible interview questions. Regardless of your level of preparedness and time spent practicing, you may encounter questions that you had no considered or expected. There's no need to be nervous though. Just try to be honest and give detailed answers, while being sure to showcase your positive attributes without seeming too braggadocios.

CHAPTER SEVEN: LETTERS OF RECOMMENDATION

An essential component of the college application are the letters of recommendation from your high school teachers, mentors, researchers you've worked with, your boss, or guidance counselors. Increasingly, admission committees are combing through these letters to gain a better insight into the type of student that you are. This is because, amongst other things, students are being coached and guided through the application process in a way that makes it difficult to truly trust the veracity of their own personal statements. The letters they receive from recommenders have not been read by the applicant, so they provide a measure of secrecy that increases the likelihood of finding out information about the student from an outside observer's point of view.

While your grades and test scores are likely to be the first and most important components of your application, admissions counselors know that these measurables and statistics can be manipulated or tell an incomplete story. Your essay and personal statement give you the opportunity to share your story and paint the picture of you as a person and you should feel free to share it with your letter writers when asking for a recommendation.

College admission committees will want an outside perspective, opinion, and judgement of your character to ensure they're offering admission to the right applicants. Who you select to submit a letter, how you ask them, when you ask them, are all small details that may affect the type of letter that gets submitted on your behalf. As you begin your application your process it is important you consider your relationship with your teachers, coaches, counselors, or employees that may be able to provide the best letter and you should consider the following list when beginning this process.

1. **Start really early**. This advice is true for all aspects of your application but it's also important to plan ahead for your letters. You need to build a strong report or relationship with someone in order for them to have enough examples and feelings in their memory bank to write you a strong letter. Simply getting an A in a teacher's class isn't enough without more interactions for them to draw upon when crafting their recommendation. You should start building these relationships as early as you can, even your first year of high school, and make sure you stay in touch with the ones you like the most and feel like you've impressed. If you need to stay after class, volunteer, or participate in clubs the teacher participates in, then you definitely should. This way, you can build a relationship out of the classroom and more in depth. Naturally, if you make a good impression, you'll have an easier time finding someone who can recommend you to your dream university!

2. **Choose wisely**. Getting an A in a teachers class will hopefully be common for you as you are planning to apply to highly selective institutions. A quiet student who never develops a relationship with their professor can get an A in a class. You need more than just a good grade to ensure you get a good letter. In fact, a class that you struggled in, persevered through, and that the teacher saw you triumph over obstacles might provide

a better opportunity for your letter writer to write a compelling letter. You should also ask directly if your guidance counselor or teacher feels comfortable writing a strong letter for you. Hopefully, they will be honest with you, but it falls upon you to make sure they are excited about writing to a college for you. You won't get to see these letters, so you'll have to feel confident that this person is going to write great things about you.

3. **Give them your details and deadlines**. This is extra work for your teachers. You're asking them to consider you as a student and human and remember all of your strengths and weaknesses. You're asking them to craft a grammatically correct and powerful statement on your behalf. Most teachers don't take this lightly so you should be as helpful as you can in order to ensure a crafty letter is submitted for you. You should give them several weeks or months of advanced notice that you will be soliciting a letter from them when you submit your applications. You should let them know when the deadlines will be, so you'll need to find out on your own and provide them with accurate information. As someone who has written countless letters for students, I can tell you it can take some time to do the job justice. Additionally, you should provide them a lot of additional information like supplying your personal essay, a list of your extracurriculars or achievements, or perhaps even a resume, and any other pertinent information so that have ideas to draw from. This will also help provide a cohesive story between your own writing and theirs. Don't be offended if they straight up ask you for this information because it doesn't mean they've forgotten you; it just means that they want to include all the information in their letter that makes you special! Be kind and considerate when asking. They're doing you a favor and you should show gratitude.

CHAPTER EIGHT: AFFORDING COLLEGE

Increasingly, students and parents alike are considering the financial impacts, ramifications, and cost of an education. These concerns are only heightened at elite universities which often charge the most exorbitant tuition and fees to their students. Soaring costs are problematic, and much debate has taken place on the value of an education, but the numbers don't lie: a college education opens doors and provides an almost guaranteed lifetime earnings increase over high school graduates. A recent study by the United States Census Bureau showed the lifetime earnings of someone with a high school degree stands at an average of $1.2 million. A Bachelor's Degree, however, brings in an average lifetime earnings of around $2.1 million. While some degrees lead to higher lifetime earnings than others, even low paying college degrees pay out more than a high school diploma. Additionally, studies have shown that having access to higher education leads to increased happiness levels, as reported by participants in a University of Pennsylvania study.

Sadly, the great recession led to decreased government spending on education and students and parents have had to make up the difference at colleges. This has led some to question to true value of a college education, but up to this point, the data support the notion that a college degree is a financially beneficial endeavor. Fortunately, here are many things you can do to diminish the rising costs of obtaining a college education and prepare to afford the college of your dreams.

Let's start with the good news: most students receive some amount of financial help in paying for college. This brings down the true cost of an education from the "sticker price" listed on school websites. For example, the average private college charges about $45,370 dollars, which includes tuition, room, and board. According to a study by The College Board, however, the average student at these colleges only paid out $26,080; notably less. At public colleges, the average cost of tuition, room, and board was significantly lower at $20,090 and the average in-state student paid around $14,000. Out of state students paid more but the cost of attending your public in-state university will likely have a lower sticker price than most private schools.

There are several different types of financial aid that help alleviate the cost of the college education and many of them will be available to most students. Navigating all of the red tape, the bureaucracy associated with them, and outdated government websites is key to gaining additional financial support to make attending your dream school more affordable. Grants are one of the forms of aid provided by colleges, states, and the federal government to meet the financial needs of students. Importantly, this form of aid doesn't need to be returned, repaid, or given back at the completion of your education. Most, admittedly, are awarded on financial need as determined by parental impact reported on the Free Application for Federal Student Aid, also known as FAFSA. According to The College Board, grants awarded to students at public colleges received an average of $5,000 in grant aid per year, and students at private colleges received around $16,700.

Colleges and states take into consideration how much they think your family can afford to pay for college based on your "estimated family contribution," or EFC, to determine the amount of aid you might receive in the form of grants. Additionally, the US government gives out what is known as a Federal Pell Grant that are capped at $5,920 per year, which goes to families most in need. Families most in need are required to earn less than $30,000 annually and any additional family income will substantially reduce the amount of federal grants that can be obtained. State grants are also vary and have different eligibility rules. Fortunately, these grants don't need to be specifically applied for, either individually or in bulk, and simply filling in tax returns for the previous year and submitting your application on the FAFSA website will automatically determine the amount of aid to be received in the form of grants.

The college that you are hoping to attend also has financial aid packages that they can extend to students, either merit-based aid or need-based aid. A little-known fact about these financial aid packages is that you can negotiate the amount of you receive. In fact, experts suggest that all students write a formal appeal letter and following up with a phone call to request more aid, regardless of the financial support the school might be offering. When haggling over the amount of aid to be received, you should always emphasize why you're a good fit for the school, whether or not you received more aid from a comparable college, and explain your financial situation that makes it clear why receiving additional support will be impactful for both you and the college. Sometimes your family has additional expenses, like medical bills, that aren't reflected on government filings and are thus unlikely to be considered without pointing them out to colleges. It is especially important to mention if your family's financial circumstances may be different than reflected on your FAFSA documentation. Since your FAFSA application is based on income from the prior year, a loss or change in job or salary might require a reassessment from the school to offer more support.

Submitting a FAFSA application also opens up the ability to participate in work-study jobs, which are part-time jobs on or nearby campus for eligible students. Eligibility is also determined by family financial contribution estimations made by FAFSA in addition to funding available at the school. Work-study jobs pay students directly for the work, based on hourly wages.

Seeking out alternative part-time jobs to help afford college is another route often pursued by students.

Thousands upon thousands of private scholarships are available on an application-by-application basis. These scholarships are distributed by private companies, nonprofits, community groups, or other organizations. They can be quite tedious to apply for and often require individual and unique written essays, but many students have found success in applying for this type of funding. An important note is that there are many predatory service companies that offer "help" in this process for a charged fee, but your high school guidance counselor should be able to direct you to free online services like Scholly that suggest scholarships you might be eligible for. NextGenVest is another reputable company that even offers free mentoring to help suggest scholarships you might be eligible for.

If you or your child is an American citizen, you can also reduce your yearly taxes after paying for tuition through the American Opportunity Tax Credit. This will allow you to reduce your taxes by up to $2,500 per child to assist with fees, books, and room and board. Parents can claim this tax credit only if their modified adjusted gross income is no higher than $90,000 if filing taxes separately or $180,000 if filing jointly with your spouse.

Loans should always be the last resort to help aid in affording college. While often an inevitability, there is certainly a reason for all the recent headlines decrying the student debt crisis. However, to afford some of the more prestigious colleges with higher sticker prices, it may be an unfortunate necessity that you or your child must take out student loans. There are private lenders and government lenders for student loans and the federal government loans should always be the first source of monetary loan offerings. The typical family uses loans to cover around 20% of college cost and there is an entire industry aimed at offering huge sums of money with varying interest rates. You may need to show around for the best rates.

Since the government should be the first avenue that you seek out for loans, you'll need to fill out the FAFSA form online even if you don't qualify for Federal Pell Grants. You can only become eligible to receive federal government loans after filling out this form. Federal loans, generally, offer the lowest interest rates with the most borrower protections, regardless of your family's credit scores and ratings. Regardless of family income, students can borrow money from the federal government. However, there are strict caveats as to how much money is offered per academic year, and important guidelines for what the money can be spent on.

Using federal loans, freshman or first-year undergraduate students can borrow up to $5,500. Occasionally students that demonstrate extreme financial need can borrow more subsidized loans that don't accrue interest until after graduation. The government uses a tiered system and the second, third, and fourth year of college offers increased amounts of loan offerings.

Another type of federal loan, called the PLUS loan, allows parents to borrow more than this amount to help their child pay for college. Unlike the previously discussed type of loan, PLUS loans do require a credit check. Additionally, they typically have higher interest rates, but they may provide more financial assistance based on a family's needs. The government confers with the school to determine how much additional money the parent can borrow, but the amount is meant to help cover the rest of cost of attendance necessary that other forms of financial aid cannot cover.

Income share agreements are a new approach to paying for college that you may be unfamiliar with due to their recent development, pioneered by school's like Purdue University, among others. Income share agreements are agreements that essentially exchange a certain percentage of one's future income for dollars that fund your education today. Unlike the debt financing described above, which typically have fixed repayment schedules and can often become burdensome to pay back, income share agreements operate by charging you a percentage of your tuition after graduation, largely based on your income after gaining employment. Because this model is so new, it remains to be seen if it is truly a 'better' option for students to afford college, but it is a growing option that you should carefully evaluate if given the opportunity to decide between this type of payment plan or traditional loan-type methods.

Private loans are also another option for students; however, they should only be explored as viable options if federal aid or other types of funding have been exhausted and remain insufficient to cover the full cost of attendance. Private school loans offer flexible interest rate options and repayment terms but often are much more rigid in their default terms. When seeking out a private student loan you should always be sure to 'shop around' for the best rates, fees, and repayment terms. Obviously, it's best to keep interest rates and fees as low as possible, but you should also look for a few other factors. Many private loan lenders do a soft pull on your credit, which will allow you to shop around without negatively impacting your credit score, long term. You should be afforded a two-week window to proceed with this rate shopping process. The most trusted private loan providers, in no particular order, are Earnest, Sallie Mae, College Ave, Common-Bond, Discover, Citizens Bank, and LendKey. There are obviously many other companies hoping to cash in on student loans, but the preceding list is a great place to begin looking, if you need to.

When deciding if a private loan is right for you and your family, you should remember that the same protections afforded by federal loans are rarely the same for private banks. Largely, they start accruing interest immediately upon disbursal, you cannot participate in federal student loan forgiveness programs, and the deferment and forbearance opportunities are often limited. It is also likely that you'll need a co-signer for private loans unless you have a strong credit history or can provide substantial collateral for the loan. If you do need a co-signer, they will also be on hook for the lifetime of the loan and you will need to convince someone that you trust, that also has a strong credit background, to agree to the terms of the loan. Used wisely, private loans can be the lifeline a student needs to gain access to the school of their dreams.

CHAPTER NINE: WHAT IF YOU GET REJECTED?

C ollege admissions can be quite competitive at any college. Presumably, you have ambitions of applying to the most elite and prestigious schools and universities. With that prestige inherently comes increased selectivity, and thus, the highest rejection rates. Even the most gifted and talented students that put together the most complete applications are never guaranteed a spot at Harvard, Yale, or Princeton. Speaking as someone who has gone through the admissions process at these selective schools and witnessing my classmates navigate the process and later serving on admissions committees, I can tell you that talent, hard work, and quality are difficult to quantify. Many decisions are difficult to make when evaluating students. What one person sees as a quality candidate, another may not. There are countless factors out of your control when applying to college. So much so that you should not be too hard on yourself if you're not successful in gaining admission to your top choice school.

As mentioned before, these schools have piles of applications from the most exciting and quality students, many of whom won't be afforded the opportunity to attend their dream school. It's important to remember that if you are competitive at one top school, you will likely be competitive at other top schools, so you may have the opportunity to attend any number of the Ivy League schools even if Harvard does reject your application. Perspective is important, even if it won't feel very good being rejected to your top choice. Following the guidelines outlined in this book should certainly help you through the process, but they do not guarantee admission.

If the gates to your dream school do appear closed to you, it is recommended that you quickly move on and focus your attention on other schools that you've applied to. Some students think that appealing decisions, or reapplying the next year, are viable options. Unfortunately, those students are almost never successful, and the end result is the same but with added headaches and loss of time or money. Attending an alternative top-ranked university should not just be seen as a consolation prize, but a chance to prove your worth and abilities in a new place. After all, I've discussed the importance of 'fit' on potential happiness upon matriculation, and you may find that you were, indeed, a better fit at another institution.

You should know that you are not alone if you must attend your second, third, fourth, or even thirteenth-choice school. Every year, millions of students must do the same. While each situation is unique, you should know that you are not a failure and you will not end up some place where everyone there is a student at their first-choice school. Your nerves and anxieties about this fact are largely universal and you'll meet other students with similar stories of disappointment. Though disheartening, it's important to remember that schools accept or reject students for a myriad of reasons that may be entirely out of your control. Yale recently posted on their admissions website that they believe about 75% of their applicants are academically qualified to handle the rigorous coursework at their school but they still only accept around 6% of applicants. There simply isn't enough room for all the qualified applicants. If you are faced with rejection, it's time to shift your focus and goals to a new institution. Get excited about the process of learning something new at a completely unexpected place!

Start researching the school you are going to attend. It's likely that you spent more time on this process at your first-choice school and missed some really amazing facts about the school that did accept you. You should get pumped to spend four years challenging yourself, making best friends, meeting future business partners, and engaging with intelligent classmates and faculty. From the most prestigious colleges on the planet, to the universities considered 'safety schools by many, you will find exciting activities and interesting people to meet.

Hopefully, during the application process, you identified and subsequently applied to numerous quality institutions. Therefore, this should not be a harrowing experience to attend a second or third-choice school. This is why I suggested making a long list and applying to a variety of colleges that fit your needs and dreams and goals. Now you get to go visit those schools to see and learn about all the amazing opportunities afforded to you at these institutions. Your lens as an admitted student will likely allow you to see the institution in a new light. You'll get to meet some of the other accepted students on preview days and find clubs or activities that may interest and challenge you during your college career.

Life leaves a lot to chance and the school that you thought would be best for you might not have been after all. You should attack your freshman year with an open mind and pursue all your varied interests, regardless of where you end up. It's likely you'll change your major or career aspirations throughout your college experience. Maybe you'll join a new club or lab that changes your future in unexpected ways. You're only a teenager after all, and you should continuously learn and be introduced to things you'd never considered before. Even if this experience is initially undesirable, you may find it is the option that produces the most growth inside of you. Most colleges will provide you with the experiences you need to grow and learn and change and you get to go to a school that wants to take you on that journey!

Your story doesn't need to conclude with a rejection. Your story can and should be one about redemption, overcoming obstacles, persevering in the face of a challenge, and achieving your long-term goals through gritty fortitude. Maybe you want to apply to medical school, or law school, or graduate school after your bachelor's degree, and the college you've identified as your "dream school" will certainly love to see how you overcame setbacks in life and attacked new challenges with fervor and excitement.

If you do decide to take a gap year, and reapply later, it's important to consider what you'll do over that time. A college won't want to hear that you moped around the house, lamenting your rejection. They will want to see a fresh perspective and growth over that year, so consider your gap year activities wisely. Maybe you can spend a year abroad or working or learning, but make sure that you have a story to tell that is compelling enough to get a college admissions board to reconsider your application in its entirety. Ideally, you'll select an activity or experience related to what you want to study in school to showcase your dedication for the subject. If you do decide to reapply to your dream school, you'll need to explain why you chose to take a year off before starting college and showcase how that experience has made you a better fit for the school and, without sounding whiny, why they should reconsider your application.

Additionally, you should also remember that transferring schools is an option for some, although the process is a little different as a transfer student than a high school senior applying to college for the first time. While many students do eventually transfer into their dream school after a year or two elsewhere, you need to ensure that you perform well wherever you do attend initially. Taking rigorous coursework and excelling at another institution will showcase your readiness to continue excelling at another school. While going to a different college first may not be the plan you initially had in mind, transferring can still be an option that may ease your decision to temporarily attend a different school. While transferring into your dream school is occasionally an option, it is not an easy one. Important statistics posted on Harvard's website indicate that they accept roughly just 1% of transfer applicants, so your chances of transferring in are actually significantly lower than entering as a freshman. You can find more admissions statistics for your school of choice, typically online, or by contacting the admissions office of each school. Generally speaking, at most elite institutions, the acceptance rates are just as bleak as those presented by Harvard University and you should only pursue this option if you feel wildly compelled to.

Made in the USA
Las Vegas, NV
25 June 2021

25399575R00039